A Source Book of Lifeboats

A Source Book of
Lifeboats

Ray Kipling

Ward Lock Limited · London

Cover: Rother class lifeboat stationed at Margate.

Frontispiece: the *Elizabeth Moore Garden* lifeboat at Bude.

First published in Great Britain in 1982
by Ward Lock Limited, 82 Gower Street,
London WC1E 6EQ, a Pentos Company.

Layout by Sheila Sherwen
House editor Suzanne Kendall

Text filmset in Univers

Printed and bound in Great Britain by
Netherwood Dalton and Co. Limited, Huddersfield

British Library Cataloguing in Publication Data

Kipling, Ray
  A source book of lifeboats.—(Source books)
  1. Lifeboats—History
  I. Title
  623.8'29   VK1473

ISBN 0-7063-6158-X

Acknowledgments

I would like to thank my colleagues in the RNLI for
their help in the preparation of this book; in particular
Heather Deane who initiated the project, Commander Peter Gladwin and Symington Macdonald for
helpful comments on the text and Olive Walker, Ros
Smalley and Marjorie Gifford for typing. Most of all, I
would like to thank the lifeboat crews, families and
station officials whose co-operation and friendship
has made this work so rewarding.

Picture credits

H. E. Appleton; S. Bennetts; Birmingham Post
& Mail; R. Bishop; British Hovercraft Corp. Ltd;
R. Clegg; Cornish Photonews; Daily Telegraph;
A. Dick; Doran Bros.; Dorset News; Downland
Studios; Eastern Daily Press; Evening Echo;
Evening Post, Jersey; Focus Press; B. Green; A.
Greenway; P. Hadfield; W. Hardy (Look & Learn); E.
Harrison; B. M. Kidd; C. MacCallum; Mobil Shipping
Co.; Motor Boat & Yachting; Northern Echo; D.
Parker; Poppyland Photographs; Press Association;
Press & Journal, Aberdeen; RAF; RNAS
Lossiemouth; RNAS Prestwick; A. W. Stubbs; D.
Trotter; C. Watson; T. Weedon; S. Wilson; Yachting
World; K. Yuill.

Contents

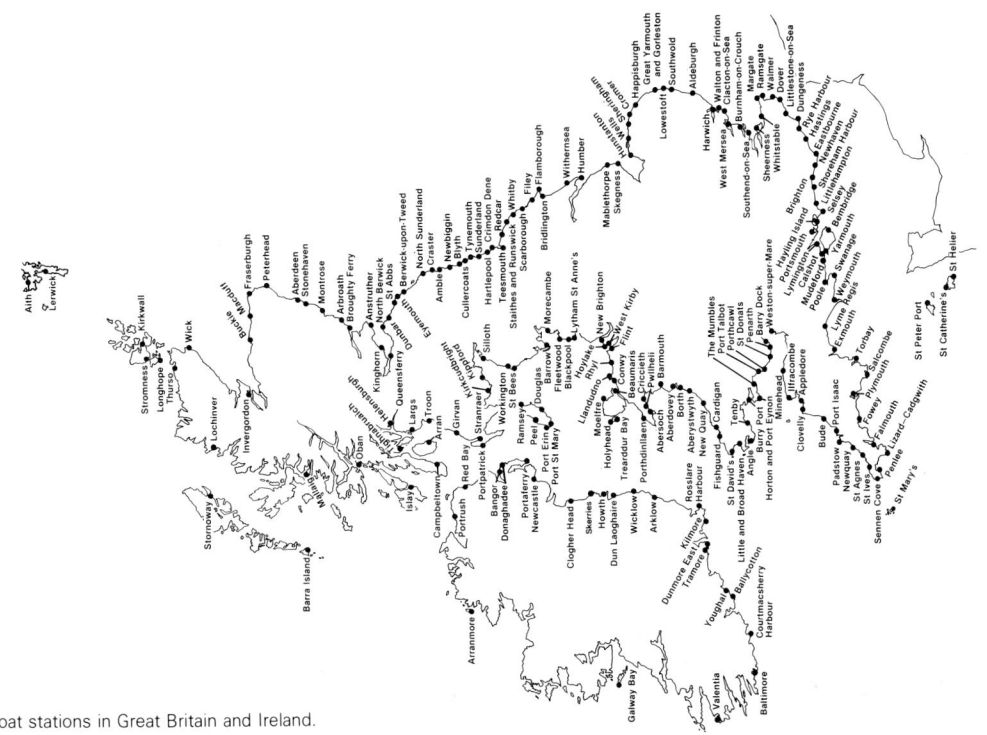

Lifeboat stations in Great Britain and Ireland.

Glossary

Ballast heavy material in boat to make it stable
Batten to fasten down with a strip of wood
Breeches buoy life buoy attached to ropes for rescue
Buoyancy capacity for floating
Drogue device towed behind lifeboat in certain conditions to steady it
Fender flexible object placed over boat's side for protection
Groyne a strong wooden structure, like a fence, built across a beach to stop erosion by the sea
Gunwhale the upper edge around the side of a boat
Keel the part of a boat extending from front to back along the bottom and supporting the whole frame
Lashed tied with a rope
Life-rocket rocket guns used to fire a line to wrecked ships
Maroon type of firework which explodes high in the air with loud bang
Mortar wide barrelled gun for firing lines or making signals
Pulling lifeboat lifeboat with oars
Spar a pole supporting sails
Stern back of a boat or ship

Thwart a cross-piece in a boat, used as seat for rowers
Warp a rope used for towing
Wheelhouse enclosed steering position on a boat

Introduction

Long before anybody thought of inventing a lifeboat, people were using the sea as a source of food and a means of transport. Sailing ships were at the mercy of the wind and for hundreds of years the only help available was from other boats in the area. Fishermen worked in fleets fairly close to the shore and could help each other to some extent. Ships on long voyages either survived or sank without trace. If they were wrecked within sight of the land they might be helped by local boatmen; if they foundered further out to sea, nothing could be done. So although some seamen were saved from drowning, hundreds were lost and often the would-be rescuers' own boats, which were only small fishing or pilot vessels, were swamped and the crews lost their lives. This continued until the late eighteenth century when the number of voyages by merchant ships and the number of wrecks increased dramatically. In some cases, people stood on the shore and watched helplessly as sailors were swept to their death from the rigging of their wrecked ships. Gradually it was realized that special rescue boats were needed and the first lifeboats were put into service.

It is impossible to tell even a fraction of the stories of the Lifeboat Service. Over 400 RNLI lifeboatmen have died because they volunteered to go to the help of complete strangers. Families have waited anxiously for their return and have faced the crushing blow of losing a father, a brother, sometimes three or four relatives. But over 100,000 lives have been saved by these men. Some rescues have needed immense skill and bravery; others have been long and tedious with endless searches in chilling cold, soaking spray and the inky blackness of a winter night. The only explanation the lifeboatmen will give is that somebody has to do the job; they certainly do not go out for money, fame or medals.

This book looks at the lifeboats, the equipment and a few of the rescues. It summarizes many millions of hours of hard work, time willingly and freely given for one purpose only—to save lives.

An Atlantic 21 inshore lifeboat 'taking off'.

History

Nobody knows which was the world's first lifeboat station. There have been claims that the Chinese had rescue boats at the mouth of the Yangtse River in the mid-eighteenth century but there is no firm evidence of this.

At Formby, in Lancashire, however, there was a boat set aside for lifesaving in the 1770s. There was also an elaborate lifesaving organization in Bamburgh, Northumberland, where, in 1772, the Crewe Trust was established to pay for men to patrol the beaches on horseback during bad storms, looking for ships in trouble. The Trust also provided a bell to act as a fog warning, a signal gun which was fired to summon help if a wreck was spotted, rooms for the shipwrecked sailors and even money to pay for the coffins and funerals of the unlucky ones.

In 1784 a coachbuilder, Lionel Lukin, who had heard of lives being lost because of boats overturning and sinking, decided to convert a fishing boat to make it 'unimmergible' or unsinkable. He did this by adding a thick belt of cork to the outside of the boat and fitting air cases along the inside. To add extra strength and stability an iron keel was built on and extra air cases, for buoyancy, were fitted at the bow and stern of the boat. The converted fishing boat was patented in 1785 and Dr John Sharp of the Crewe Trust bought one in 1786 to establish a lifeboat station in Bamburgh.

Three years later there was a terrible shipwreck in the mouth of the River Tyne and the whole crew of the ship *Adventure* died within full view of thousands of people on the shore who had no way of helping. A group of Newcastle businessmen offered a prize for the best plan or model of a rescue boat 'calculated to brave the dangers of the sea, particularly of broken water'. The best model was made by William Wouldhave, a local parish clerk. By using a straight keel, high ends and watertight cases containing cork, Wouldhave's design was self-righting and unsinkable. He was only offered half the prize and another man who had submitted a model, Henry Greathead, was asked to build a lifeboat using the best features of Wouldhave's design. Greathead was a local boatbuilder and gave his boat a curved keel but used Wouldhave's idea of cork-filled cases for extra buoyancy. This boat was the first ever to be designed and built specifically as a lifeboat and was called *The Original*. She was pointed at each end and could be rowed in either direction, avoiding the dangerous move of turning around, putting the boat parallel to the breaking waves and making her vulnerable to capsize. However, because he had

altered Wouldhave's design, Greathead's *Original* was not a self-righter. She had no rudder and was steered by two oars which were trailed over the stern.

Greathead built over thirty lifeboats to this design, improving them as he went on. The oldest surviving lifeboat in the world, *The Zetland,* which is still preserved in a museum in Redcar, was built by Greathead and was stationed at Redcar from 1802 to 1864, saving over 500 lives.

Meanwhile Lionel Lukin was working in Suffolk, taking local boat designs and modifying them to

Launch of the Formby, Lancashire, lifeboat about 1914. The station was opened in the 1770s and may have been the first lifeboat station in the world.

build lifeboats which suited the local seamen. One of Lukin's lifeboats was paid for by the Suffolk Humane Society and Lloyds, the marine insurers, paid for 14 of Greathead's boats.

Thus during the early 1800s lifeboat stations were being established at intervals around the coasts of the British Isles, to be run by local societies.

Henry Greathead's lifeboat *The Original* had a wide beam and thick
cork belting around the outside to give stability.

The oldest surviving lifeboat, the *Zetland,* was built by Greathead. During her service life the cork belting was removed and relieving tubes, to clear away water, were added.

One of these early stations was opened in 1802 at Douglas in the Isle of Man. A member of its crew was Sir William Hillary, a man of great courage who took part in some spectacular lifeboat rescues. He was appalled at the lack of proper lifeboat coverage all around the coast and at the unnecessary loss of life and proposed the formation of a National Institution for the Preservation of Life from Shipwreck. He gathered support from influential people in London, including Members of Parliament, the Archbishop of Canterbury and the Lord Mayor of London, and on 4 March 1824 the Institution was founded. Hillary's plans were so accurate that they are still in use today. He proposed local committees to run the lifeboat station with '. . . crews selected from the bravest and most experienced persons who can be found. Volunteers should be invited to enrol themselves from amongst the resident pilots, seamen, fishermen, boatmen and others. To expect a large body of men to enrol themselves and be in constant readiness to risk their own lives for the preservation of those whom they have never known or seen,

perhaps of another nation, merely because they are fellow creatures in extreme peril, is to pay the highest possible compliment to my countrymen.' Finding the money to run the Institution presented no problem in Hillary's eyes, for he wrote '. . . who is there to whom such an Institution once become known would refuse his aid? It is a cause which extends from the palace to the cottage, in which politics and party cannot have any share . . .'

The Shipwreck Institution, as the new body was popularly known, had a good start and bought twelve new lifeboats in its first year but donations soon diminished. Grace Darling's rescue in 1838 revived public interest in sea rescue, and did help the Institution, though not greatly. Grace and her father, William, who was a lighthouse keeper on the Farne Islands, saw a wrecked steamer, *The Forfarshire,* and together they rowed their tiny boat through a gale to rescue nine survivors. Her brother and local lifeboatmen put out from the mainland but were beaten to the wreck by Grace and William. Grace, who was only 23, became a national heroine and she and her father were awarded the Shipwreck Institution's silver bravery medal. The Institution itself soon entered a very bad period and 1841 to 1850 no appeal was made for funds. Many lifeboats were neglected and became unseaworthy and it took a

Grace Darling's famous rescue from the wrecked steamer *Forfarshire,* Grace and her father rescued 9 survivors, many more had already drowned.

disaster at South Shields in 1849, when the lifeboat capsized drowning twenty out of her crew of twenty-four, to revitalize the Institution.

A new secretary was appointed and in 1851 The Duke of Northumberland became President and launched a new competition for the best model of a lifeboat. This was a turning point for the Lifeboat Service which has never looked back.

The Duke's competition attracted 280 entries from all over the country, with three models from America and two from the Netherlands. Many were very imaginative, if rather impractical and the ideas included the use of corrugated iron and perforated zinc as building materials, manpower to turn paddles, a raft with hydrogen filled tubes and a collapsible structure made of wickerwork covered with canvas which could be rolled along the beach to the site of the wreck and then opened out into a boat.

The judges decided to award each model points based on its different qualities. The maximum score was 100 points, made up as follows:

Qualities as a rowing boat in all weathers	20
Qualities as a sailing boat	18
Qualities as a sea boat; as stability, safety, buoyancy forward for launching through a surf, &c	10
Small internal capacity for water up to the level of the thwarts	9
Means of freeing boat of water readily	8
Extra buoyancy; its nature, amount, distribution, and mode of application	7
Power of self-righting	6
Suitableness for beaching	4
Room for, and power of, carrying passengers	3
Moderate weight for transport along shore	3
Protection from injury to the bottom	3
Ballast, as iron 1, water 2, cork 3	3
Access to stem or stern	3
Timber heads, for securing warps to	2
Fenders, life-lines, &c	1
	100

It is interesting that sailing was not considered as important as rowing; the view then was that as rowing was used more generally around the coasts, and sailing only in certain areas, such as Norfolk and Suffolk, the rowing qualities of the boat were the most important.

The winner of the competition was James Beeching whose model was awarded 84 points; 35 other models scored over 60 points.

A typical self-righting pulling and sailing lifeboat of the 1860s. The design is based on Beeching's, with air cases at bow and stern.

Beeching's boat was 11 m (36 ft) long and had a thick belt of cork around it and air cases inside for buoyancy. A ballast tank in the bottom of the boat held 2¼ tons of water and a heavy iron keel helped the stability. The raised air cases at the bow and stern combined with the water ballast and keel to make the boat self-righting; if she capsized she would float on the air cases and be pulled back upright by the leverage of the keel and water ballast. Sea water getting into the boat was cleared by 'delivering valves', tubes which would let the water run straight out of the boat but not back in again. The boat had twelve oars and two sails; she could carry up to seventy people and cost £250.

Beeching built a few lifeboats to his design but the committee had recommended some improvements and asked James Peake, one of their members, to incorporate the good qualities from all the models to make a new lifeboat. The result was a 9.1 m (30 ft) self-righting lifeboat which formed the basis for the RNLI fleet for the next fifty years. It was continually improved and modified but was not the only design

used; in East Anglia, for example, much larger sailing boats were favoured.

The Duke of Northumberland's committee also made a thorough review of all lifeboats, life-rockets (rocket guns used to fire a line to wrecked ships) and mortars around the coasts. Many of the lifeboats were still run by local associations and it was clear that many were in such a bad condition that they needed replacing. The committee had therefore achieved a great deal in showing the need for a plan for the Institution's future.

Several of the competition entrants had suggested that steam power should be used in lifeboats. This was rejected, though many lifeboat rescues were carried out by a paddle steamer towing the lifeboat out to the wreck; the lifeboat was then released, rowed or sailed to pick up the survivors and returned to the steamer to be towed back to station.

One of the most outstanding rescues by a tug and lifeboat was in 1881, when the ship *Indian Chief* ran aground in a gale on Long Sand, a sandbank off the Thames Estuary. Lifeboats from Aldeburgh, Clacton and Harwich to the north of the Thames and Rams-gate to the south all set out at midday. Long Sand is about 48·3 km (30 miles) from Ramsgate and the tug *Vulcan* with the lifeboat *Bradford* in tow took almost five hours to reach the area. The seas were so rough

The lifeboat *Hope* was stationed at Appledore from 1862 to 1890 and lived up to her name by saving 59 lives.

20

The tug *Vulcan* towing the Ramsgate lifeboat *Bradford* to the wreck of the *Indian Chief*. Every man on the lifeboat and the tug was awarded a bravery medal for this rescue which lasted 26 hours.

that the coxswain, Charles Fish later said that *Vulcan* was thrown up like a ball, and her starboard paddle came clear of the water high enough for a coach to pass underneath. The tow was head to wind and within minutes the lifeboatmen were soaked and any shelter they tried to rig was immediately blown away.

By 5 pm night was closing in and Kentish Knock Lightship was sighted. The men gave a bearing for the wreck and then signals from Sunk Lightship were seen, but the wreck could not be found in the darkness. Although they were already cold, soaked and tired, the lifeboatmen and the crew of the tug resolved to stay by Long Sand until dawn.

For the next fourteen hours the lifeboatmen sought what little comfort they could find as the waves swept over their open boat in the howling gale. As the lifeboat pitched and tossed, ten men would huddle together for warmth, while two, secured by lifelines, acted as lookouts.

As dawn rose, one of the crew spotted the wreck and the lifeboat immediately cast off her tow rope and hoisted her sails. The seas around Long Sand were a boiling fury and had carried away all but the foremast of *Indian Chief*. The master and sixteen of his crew had perished during the night and their bodies were tangled in the wreckage of spars, rigging and torn canvas. With great difficulty the lifeboat came in close to the wreck and as seas swept right over her the survivors were taken aboard, one by one. The lifeboat then set out to rejoin the tug through such fearful seas that some of the rescued men thought that perhaps they had been safer lashed to the rigging of the wreck.

Eventually, *Vulcan* and *Bradford* entered Ramsgate Harbour, 26 hours after setting out, to be met by a crowd who could hardly believe the physical suffering and anguish on the survivors' faces. Stirring accounts of the rescue appearing in *The Daily Telegraph* were an inspiration to the whole nation, and the gold medal of the Institution was awarded to Coxswain Charles Fish, while the silver medal was awarded to each of his crew as well as to the master, engineer and crew members of the tug *Vulcan*.

The difficulties of fitting small boats with a coal burning steam engine were considerable but by 1887 the RNLI felt confident enough to announce another competition—this time to offer medals for 'drawings or models of a mechanically propelled lifeboat best adapted to meet the conditions under which lifeboats are called upon to perform their work'. In fact no awards were made, but shortly afterwards a steam lifeboat was ordered. The new boat was to use hydraulic propulsion with a powerful pump sucking in seawater and ejecting it through nozzles in the side of the boat—water jet propulsion. Paddle wheels were not practical for a small boat and conventional propellers were rejected due to the likelihood of damage and tangling in wreckage.

The first steam lifeboat *Duke of Northumberland,* was built in 1890. She was a steel boat 15·2 m (50 ft) long with an average speed of 7 knots and cost £5,000. It took 20 to 25 minutes to get up steam from cold, or 15 minutes if the boiler had been warmed. The boat weighed 30 tons and had to be moored afloat in the sheltered water of a harbour. She proved very successful and two more hydraulic steam lifeboats were built for the RNLI and one for the South Holland Lifeboat Society. Having gained experience with steam propulsion, the RNLI decided that a conventional propeller would make the lifeboat faster, and a new design was worked out with a tunnel in the hull to protect the propeller. One of these lifeboats was sent to Padstow and in April 1900 she was setting out on a rescue when a huge wave rolled over her, capsized her and washed her up, completely wrecked, on the rocks. She was replaced by a sailing lifeboat but a special steam tug, the only one ever built by the RNLI, was sent to Padstow to tow the lifeboat in bad conditions. The steam lifeboats did good work and showed that engine power could achieve far more than men's muscles. In 1908, the Holyhead steam lifeboat, *Duke of Northumberland,* was called out to help a steamer in a gale and, on returning to her station it was learned that another steamer was in difficulties, drifting towards the rocky shores of Anglesey. The lifeboat set out into the storm, which had increased to a hurricane with winds of 129 km/h (80 mph) and huge seas. The power of the steam lifeboat forced her through the waves in conditions that would have been too severe for any pulling or sailing boat. When she reached the steamer, the seas were so violent that the lifeboat was tossed around like a cork and it was two hours before the coxswain could get near enough to throw a rope to the survivors. Seven men were dragged to safety when a huge wave swept the lifeboat towards the wreck. The last two men jumped on to the lifeboat which was immediately driven clear by the coxswain. Throughout the rescue the lifeboat was in danger of being smashed against the side of the steamer which would have killed the crew. Coxswain William Owen won the gold medal for the rescue and his crew all won silver medals.

The steam lifeboats might have lasted longer if they had not been overtaken by the arrival of the internal combustion engine at the beginning of the twentieth century.

The Padstow steam lifeboat (above) sets out on a rescue in 1899. She was capsized and wrecked a year later and was replaced by a steam tug and pulling and sailing lifeboat (right).

The RNLI's first attempt to produce a motor lifeboat was in 1904 when a 9 kW (12 hp) petrol engine was fitted to an old lifeboat. The trials were promising and a speed of 6 knots was achieved. More powerful engines were fitted to other boats and, as the trials continued it was decided to design a lifeboat especially to take an engine. At this stage, the engine was still auxilliary to sails as marine petrol engines were not very reliable but steady progress was made to build more motor lifeboats and just as the steam lifeboats had shown the value of power, the petrol-engined lifeboats soon proved themselves. In 1914 a hospital ship, The Rohilla with 224 people on board, was driven ashore off Whitby and after two gallant launches by the Whitby No. 2 lifeboat, thirty-five people were saved. The boat was too badly damaged to put out again and the Upgang lifeboat, after being lowered down the cliffs on ropes, tried to reach the wreck but could not get close enough to save anybody. The Scarborough

lifeboat was towed to the scene by a steam trawler but could not reach the *Rohilla* and the Teesmouth lifeboat sprang a leak as she was being towed down the coast. Whitby's No. 1 lifeboat was launched but to no effect so, after attempts by five pulling lifeboats, the new motor lifeboat at Tynemouth was summoned. In the turmoil of the seas the motor lifeboat approached the wreck and, in spite of completely disappearing when the waves swept over her, rescued the fifty survivors still left on *The Rohilla*.

Engine power had proved itself and by the RNLI's centenary in 1924, one-fifth of the fleet were motor lifeboats. The largest pulling and sailing lifeboat at this time was the 13·1 m (43 ft) Watson, weighing 11 tons. The largest motor lifeboat was the twin screw 18·3 m (60 ft) Barnett, weighing 40 tons; she was introduced in 1923 and was the first lifeboat dependent solely on her engines.

The effect of motor lifeboats on the fleet was dramatic. It was calculated that two motor lifeboats

Newburgh lifeboat landing survivors from the Aberdeen trawler, *Imperial Prince,* in 1923. In a huge rescue operation a line was fired over the wreck by rocket apparatus on the shore but the survivors were too exhausted to haul it in. The Aberdeen lifeboat was launched but was swept back on to the shore. The Peterhead motor lifeboat set out to help but by the time she arrived the Newburgh lifeboat had been dragged 11 km (7 miles) along the beach and, in four separate attempts, managed to rescue 7 men.

The wrecked hospital ship *Rohilla* at Whitby with a pulling lifeboat which attempted to help. The new motor lifeboat from Tynemouth carried out the final rescue.

Pulling lifeboats (above left) and pulling and sailing lifeboats (above right) were being replaced by motor lifeboats in the 1920s the largest of which was the 18·3 m (60 ft) Barnett (left).

were equivalent to five pulling and sailing lifeboats. They could go faster and further in worse conditions; they could save lives which, without them, would be lost. Less stations were needed, but each one cost more for the motor boats, being heavier, often needed new boathouses and slipways. The boats themselves were much more expensive and required constant maintenance, so a full-time mechanic had to be employed at each station. Before motors were introduced, no protection was provided for the crews, but motor lifeboats incorporated cabins and shelters, for the crews were staying out longer and travelling further. Less crew members were needed as the engines, rather than the men, provided the power.

In 1934 experiments with diesel engines started and these led to the present twin diesel-engined lifeboats; the Liverpools, Watsons, Barnetts and much later, to the Waveneys and Aruns.

World War II put a considerable strain on the RNLI. Young men were called up to fight, leaving many lifeboat crews short and retired crew members returned to man the boats. Maroons could not be fired to call out the crews and there were no floodlights for night launches. At sea there were mines, submarines and aircraft to contend with and the lifeboats had to navigate without the help of coast

The small motor lifeboats still carried sails. This is a motor self-righter built in 1936 and stationed at Port St Mary, Isle of Man.

lights which were all extinguished. The number of calls on the lifeboat service increased dramatically as ships and aircraft were attacked and blown up. Men were rescued irrespective of nationality although the RNLI was criticized for saving German airmen. In reply the Institution pointed out that since its foundation it had helped all nationalities, in war and peace, and said 'That high rule of conduct has been scrupulously observed by the lifeboat service for 117 years.' On a more sinister note the Air Ministry encouraged the saving of German airmen by British boats so that the prisoners could be questioned and prevented from returning home to fly again.

The total number of lifeboat launches during the war was 3,760, of which 2,212 were to war casualties. Almost half of these were to aircraft, though out of a total of six thousand lives saved during the war, only 142 were from aircraft. One airman who was rescued by the Margate lifeboat was a young fighter pilot, Richard Hillary, the great great great great nephew of the RNLI's founder Sir William Hillary.

The lifeboat service had never been so busy and with a large number of rescues in appalling weather, thirteen lifeboatmen died. Three of these were direct casualties of the war, one man being killed when a German plane machine-gunned the St Peter Port lifeboat and two men being blown up by a mine off Minehead. Six lifeboats were lost, four from bombings, and two from war action. The Channel Islands were occupied by the Germans but the St Helier lifeboat continued with her work and saved thirty-five lives. A Belgian lifeboat joined the RNLI Fleet for most of the war, returning to Belgium in 1946. Three lifeboats were taken over by the Government for special lifesaving duties and had to be replaced by relief boats.

Incredible bravery was shown by the wartime lifeboat crews, though their enemy was the sea not man. Time after time the veteran lifeboat crews put out to help sinking ships and battled against almost impossible odds. The RNLI awarded eight gold, forty-three silver and 153 bronze medals for gallantry. The gold medal rescues are so fantastic as to be almost unbelievable. Coxswain Robert Cross of Humber, who saved 244 lives in four years of the war, won two of the gold medals for rescues in conditions which nearly wrecked his lifeboat; in Ireland, Coxswain John Boyle of Arranmore took four hours to rescue eighteen men from a Dutch steamer in a hurricane and Coxswain Patrick Murphy of Newcastle, Co. Down, rescued thirty-nine men by driving his lifeboat through a channel little wider than the boat itself; the legendary Coxswain Henry Blogg of Cromer won his third gold medal for saving eighty-

19 lifeboats took part in the evacuation from Dunkirk in June 1940. The Eastbourne lifeboat, *Jane Holland,* was taken across the English Channel by the Navy and was found abandoned sometime later, severely damaged. The Navy repaired her and returned her to the RNLI. The bullet-ridden ventilating pipe is on display in the Eastbourne lifeboat museum.

During World War II, lifeboats still had to deal with their normal casualties, such as this sailing barge in difficulties off Margate in 1939, being assisted by the Margate lifeboat *Lord Southborough* which landed 23 survivors (one badly injured).

eight lives from four steamers wrecked on sand-banks, sailing his lifeboat over the decks of two of the ships; in Scotland, Coxswain John McLean of Peterhead saved 106 lives from three steamers in gales of 169 km/h (105 mph) in a service lasting seventy-five hours; in Wales, Coxswain William Gammon, who later died in the Mumbles lifeboat disaster of 1947, rescued forty-two men from a Canadian frigate with two men of over seventy in his lifeboat crew; Lieutenant Bennison of Hartlepool found his lifeboat almost standing on end as he rescued the crew of a steamer which had broken into two pieces.

The war, however, brought lifeboat construction to a virtual standstill. A pre-war plan to build twenty-nine new lifeboats was resumed in 1945 and a new plan was made to build fifty more new boats. These were the Liverpools, Watsons and Barnetts, the lifeboat classes which are now disappearing from the fleet, to be replaced by faster, more powerful, craft.

From *The Original* to the Arun was a gigantic step; the pulling lifeboat had 2·2 kW (3 hp), the modern lifeboat 686 kW (920 hp). Although the boats have changed dramatically, their crews face the same storms. Technology has made their job safer than ever before but nothing can change the weather.

The last pulling lifeboat, *Robert and Ellen Robson,* (above) was stationed at Whitby until 1957 mainly for work inside the harbour and is now on display in Whitby's lifeboat museum. One of her predecessors, *Jacob and Rachel Valentine,* was used to rescue two ladies cut off when the River Esk flooded in 1931. The lifeboat (opposite) was taken by road to Ruswarp, pulled by horses and is seen here after the rescue, returning to Whitby.

Modern lifeboats

The coastline of Britain and Ireland is one of the most varied in the world with high cliffs, rocky bays, long sandy beaches, river estuaries and man-made harbours. This means that different types of lifeboat are needed, some to work close to the shore and near sandbanks and others to go far out to sea. Launching can also be a problem and often dictates the type of lifeboat needed. So the modern lifeboat fleet is composed of a mixture of designs, as the following pages show.

Design

Lifeboats are designed in the RNLI's own drawing offices, sometimes from scratch and sometimes starting from a hull shape which has been designed by an outside consultant. Lifeboat design poses some unique problems. The boats must be small enough to get close to wrecks, strong enough to go to sea in the worst weather, well equipped with navigation, communication and survival gear, stable enough to make capsize unlikely and self-righting in case they should be capsized. The draughtsmen may also have to limit the size and weight of new lifeboats so that they will fit into existing boathouses or on to launching carriages. The first step is to draw the hull, then to make a scale model which can be tested in special test tanks where artificial waves are made. The model is also tested at sea and by observing and filming its behaviour and comparing it with other models, the designers can correct any faults. For example, the model might roll too much, or might not clear away spray so that the coxswain would not be able to see where he was going. While the model trials are being carried out, another team of draughtsmen is working out precisely where every piece of equipment will go in the hull and what it will all weigh. The engines are the biggest and heaviest items and must be placed as low as possible in the hull to give it stability. Lifeboats have two diesel engines so that if one is damaged, or its propeller is fouled, the other can carry on. Fuel tanks are also placed low down in the hull and again two tanks are used in case one is damaged. Generators provide power for all the electrical and electronic equipment and each electrical circuit is made as short as possible so that if one piece of equipment is damaged it will not interfere with anything else. The lifeboat hulls are sub-divided into watertight sections and with reserve buoyancy provided by air cases or foam blocks, they are virtually unsinkable.

Every item must now be added with great care to ensure that it is in exactly the right place. Equipment

A model of an Arun class lifeboat hull is tested in a tank. It is travelling at the equivalent of 20 knots and throwing up too much water. The solution was to fit spray rails.

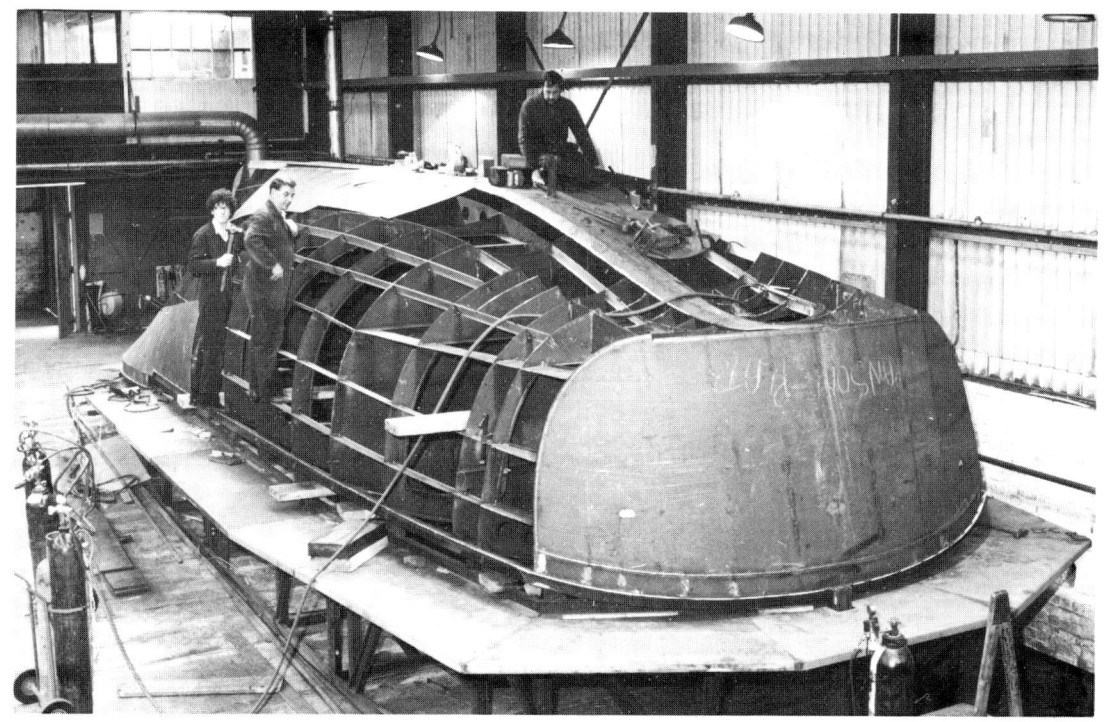

must be accessible but well secured so that it does not come loose in rough weather. Only when the designers and technicians have thoroughly checked their drawings can building begin.

Construction

The traditional way of building a lifeboat was to build a wooden frame of elm or oak, steaming and bending the timbers to give the curved shape of the hull. Mahogany or teak planks were then fixed diagonally to this framework and covered with calico coated with white lead. A second layer of planks was then fixed to run diagonally, but at right angles to the first layer. This meant that the grain of the first plank ran opposite to that of the second, giving great strength and flexibility. Early Rother class boats, which are the last class of traditional shaped lifeboats built in wood, had a similar construction, starting with a keel of teak and building up a skeleton frame of oak with mahogany spacers. But now there are three layers of planks, bent into position and glued in a process called cold moulding. The laminate of three layers is then screwed and nailed to the frame for extra strength.

Steel lifeboats are built quite differently and the

Welding steel plates to the hull of the fast slipway lifeboat.

fast slipway lifeboat is actually built upside down with the order of construction reversed. The gunwhale is laid down and the watertight bulkheads are erected before the steel frame and keel are welded in. Steel plates are then welded to the frame to form the hull and this is the stage where it is easier to build the boat upside down, as the welder can look down on his work rather than reaching up to it. The steel hull is then turned right way up for the fitting of equipment and the wheelhouse.

The third material used for lifeboat hulls is glass reinforced plastic (GRP) or glass fibre. This is made of two components. Thin strands of glass are woven together to make a material similar to sacking; coarse, flexible and strong. This is made hard and rigid by covering it with a plastic resin. The glass fibre is built up in layers, with resin being added in between each layer to form a tough GRP hull. Different types of glass fibre are used in alternate layers to give special strength and the hull is made in a giant wooden mould which is removed when all the layers are complete.

Once the wooden, steel or GRP hull has been made, the fitting out takes place. This means making the wheelhouse and cabins, installing the engines, gearboxes and propellers and all the other equipment. It takes up to two years to build each lifeboat.

A glass reinforced plastic Arun hull is inspected by the RNLI's chief
technical officer after the wooden mould (left) has been taken away.

Trials

Every new lifeboat has a long programme of trials, to test all the machinery and equipment. Speed trials, engine trials, inclining tests all have to be satisfactory before the boat goes to her station. All lifeboats share the qualities of strength and reliability and now all are built to be self-righting. This means that if the lifeboat is turned over by a large wave she will automatically come back up. To test this the lifeboat is hauled over by a huge crane until she is upside down. The rope is then released and the lifeboat automatically rights herself, in 4 to 10 seconds. The latest lifeboats are self-righting because the superstructure contains air with watertight doors keeping the sea out. The superstructure is then like a giant balloon, which, if held underwater, will force its way up because of the air trapped inside. With the lifeboat, this means that she could float upside down, but the narrowness of the superstructure compared with the breadth of the hull and the weight and leverage of the engines make her unstable in this position and she is rolled around to come upright again

The modern lifeboat fleet

The idea of self-righting goes back to the days of William Wouldhave but early self-righting boats were less stable than the non-self-righters, and therefore more likely to capsize, so they were not liked by the crews.

By 1958 there were only five self-righters left in the fleet. In that year the first modern self-righter, an 11·3 m (37 ft) boat, designed by Richard Oakley, was introduced. This boat relies on water ballast for her righting; seawater is taken into tanks at the bottom of the boat when she launches, and if she is capsized the water transfers to tanks in the side of the lifeboat, causing her to right herself. The Oakley became very popular with crews and a new age of self-righting began. A larger version, 14·8 m (48½ ft) long, was introduced in 1963, and then a method was found of making this lifeboat right without using the water ballast system which had valves needing careful maintenance. The new version relied on a watertight aluminium superstructure. The lifeboat was built with a steel hull and named the Solent class. As a large lifeboat she was suitable for slipway launching or for lying afloat on moorings. When the 37 ft Oakley was re-designed to take radar mounted on a watertight superstructure the resulting Rother class lifeboat became the only boat in the fleet which could be kept at any station, launching down a slipway, from a carriage, down skids laid across a beach, or lying afloat.

Self-righting trials of the Arun class lifeboat, BP Forties. The watertight superstructure is buoyant and forces the boat to right in seconds. *Opposite*

The propellers of conventional lifeboats are protected by tunnels but this limits the speed of the boats to 8 to 9 knots. *Above*

The 13·4 m (44 ft) lifeboat (above left) bought from the United States Coast Guard in 1966 had a speed of 15 knots but no propeller protection (right).

All these lifeboats have their propellers in tunnels which provide protection against hitting rocks, sandbanks or floating wreckage. The propellers are also placed well forward of the stern, and are therefore always in the water even in very rough seas, and racing of the engines is prevented. The drawback of tunnels is that until recently they limited the speed of the boat to 8 or 9 knots.

In 1966 the RNLI bought a 13·4 m (44 ft) lifeboat from the United States Coast Guard. This had a top speed of 15 knots, almost twice as fast as the conventional lifeboats. After taking the lifeboat on trials right around the coasts of Britain and Ireland and over to Holland, the RNLI slightly modified the design and named the class Waveney. These steel-hulled lifeboats have an aluminium superstructure with inherent self-righting provided by the watertight cabins. The lifeboat must lie afloat and although there is no protection for her propellers, coxswains of Waveneys have carried out spectacular rescues in shoal waters. The Waveney heralded the era of modern fast lifeboats.

By the end of the 1960s, good progress was being made with self-righting lifeboats which composed nearly a quarter of the fleet. Two disasters causing the deaths of thirteen lifeboatmen threw the need for self-righters into sharp focus, and the RNLI decided to double its boatbuilding programme with the aim of making the whole fleet self-righting by 1980.

Technicians started a research programme to convert the Watson and Barnett lifeboats and came up with an ingenious idea. By fitting a bag which would be automatically inflated by compressed air if the boat capsized, they gave the boats an emergency self-righting system. The Barnett lifeboats have always been regarded by their crews as the finest sea boats in the fleet so the news of the capsize of Barra Island's 15·9 m (52 ft) Barnett lifeboat in 1979 was greeted with some surprise. But the lifeboat was fitted with the emergency air bag and came upright in seconds with the crew suffering no more than cuts and bruises. The same night, Islay's 15·2 m (50 ft) Thames lifeboat was capsized and righted immediately, again with only superficial injuries to the crew.

The Thames class lifeboat is a development of the Waveney, almost a stretched version of the 13·4 m (44 ft) boat. She has a steel hull and aluminium superstructure like the Waveney, but has a watertight wheelhouse and is faster with a maximum speed of 18 knots. There are only two boats of this class and they have proved themselves to be fine additions to the fleet of fast afloat boats (FABs).

The Fraserburgh lifeboat *Duchess of Kent* (above left) is seen to the left of the fishing vessel just prior to capsize and (above right) as a huge wave capsizes the lifeboat, which can be seen as a dark shape to the right of the fishing vessel's mast.

Testing the emergency air bag righting system invested for Watson and Barnett lifeboats. An automatically operated valve releases compressed gas to inflate the air bag as soon as the boat is capsized. *Opposite*

The other type of FAB is the Arun class, developed during the 1970s. The first Arun was built with a wooden hull and after extensive trials which took the boat as far as Spain, several modifications were introduced, the main one being to sweep the decks down closer to the water in the middle of the boat to make it easier to pull survivors out of the water. A third Arun was built in wood with a rounded stern, then the boats were made in glass reinforced plastic (GRP) becoming the world's first large GRP lifeboats. After a number of the boats had been built with rounded sterns it was decided to go back to the square stern, taking the hull length back to 15·8 m (52 ft).

The advantages of the fast Waveney, Thames and Arun lifeboats are not only their speed in reaching the casualty but also the protection they give to their

In 1979 Barra Island's Barnett lifeboat righted successfully due to her air bag system. The air bag remains inflated. A Royal Navy Sea King helicopter lifts off a crew member. *Left*

The first Arun, 52-01, at sea with a Barnett class lifeboat. The two boats are the same length, but are obviously very different. The Arun, at 17 knots, is twice as fast as the Barnett. Her straight deck line makes it difficult to haul people out of the water and this was changed in later Aruns. *Right*

crews. Instead of a long, cold, exhausting trip, the lifeboatmen can keep warm and dry in the cabin and arrive in better condition than previously.

The largest modern lifeboat is the 21·3 m (70 ft) steel Clyde, a long-range vessel which is fully equipped with crews' quarters and a galley and can remain at sea for prolonged periods as a self contained unit. The Clyde carries two inflatable dinghies for work close inshore. All the Arun and Thames class carry inflatables and they are used on some Waveneys, Rothers and Oakleys. The Waveneys, Thames, Aruns and Clydes also carry inflatable liferafts.

Inflatables, then, are important ancillary equipment on large lifeboats. But small inflatable lifeboats are vital independent lifesavers and actually rescue more lives than the large lifeboats. The RNLI introduced 4·9 m (16 ft) inflatable boats, powered by a single outboard petrol engine, in 1963 having studied the successful use of these boats in France. The reason was that so many calls were coming comparitively close to the beach or cliffs, in reasonable weather, that the conventional lifeboats were

Launching an inflatable boat from an Arun lifeboat. *Left*

Port Isaac's inflatable lifeboat goes in amongst surf and rocks which no other lifeboat could reach. *Right*

not the best boats for the job. By the time the maroons had been fired, the crew gathered and the boat launched, one of the new inflatables could be at the scene of the rescue. The inflatables started to operate during the summer months only and soon their 20 knot speed showed them to be an essential part of the lifeboat fleet. The RNLI adapted the inflatables, putting in inner tubes and sub-dividing the tubes into sections so that if one part was deflated the boat would still float. In many cases new young recruits were needed as these boats gave their crews quite a shaking and an age limit of forty-five was imposed. The volunteers soon found that a high degree of skill was needed to handle the inflatables in choppy seas, surf and amongst rocks.

Having entered the field of small fast rescue boats, the RNLI experimented with several designs such as the Hatch boat, the Dell Quay Dory and the McLachlan. This willingness to try new ideas led to one of the most exciting and important lifeboat developments for many years, the Atlantic 21. Here was a new concept, pioneered by Rear Admiral

Tramore inflatable lifeboat made three attempts to reach this boy trapped on a rock. Each time the waves surging into the cove threw the boat away from the rocks but the boy, who had been stranded for 2 hours, was grabbed at the third attempt.

Desmond Hoare at Atlantic College, of a rigid wooden hull topped with an inflatable tube, or sponson. The hull shape allowed the boat to be pushed through the water by her twin outboard engines at higher speeds than the normal inflatable and the sponson added stability. The boat was developed in the Isle of Wight by the RNLI's Cowes Base to become a very sophisticated small craft. Atlantic 21s now have a righting system based on the principle of the gas inflated air bag, which is mounted on a frame at the stern of the boat, and the outboard engines are waterproofed using patented inventions devised by RNLI technicians. The boats have a speed of 30 knots and are now built with GRP hulls. The crew have seats in the centre of the boat and the helmsman steers with one hand on the wheel whilst adjusting the throttles with the other hand. In this way he can avoid difficult seas by going around them or racing ahead of them. The Atlantic 21s have attracted attention world-wide and several overseas lifeboat societies have bought a number of them. In calm weather the Atlantic 21, like the inflatable, looks like a fun boat but skilful handling and experience are needed in rough conditions.

The Atlantic 21 is not designed to meet the very worst sea conditions and a larger rigid inflatable, the Medina, has been designed by the team that

The Atlantic 21 is powered by two outboard engines, specially waterprooted with a system invented by RNLI engineers. The electrical systems are also waterproof so that, if the boat is capsized and righted, the engines can be restarted immediately at the push of a button. *Opposite and this page*

52

developed the Atlantic. The first two Medinas have a wooden hull and large sponson but are powered by twin inboard diesel engines, like all large lifeboats. The prototype Medina had an open steering position but a wheelhouse has been added to the second of the class.

A parallel development to the Medina is the Brede class, based on a commercial boat used by fishermen and harbour pilots. The boat has been made self-righting by watertighting the wheelhouse. She is fitted with twin engines and her hull and wheelhouse have been strengthened and a lot of extra equipment fitted to bring her up to lifeboat standards.

The major new lifeboat of the 1980s is the fast slipway lifeboat, a steel hulled vessel which launches down a slipway and has a top speed of over 15 knots. This boat was difficult to design as slipway boats must have protected propellers, built into tunnels, and this limits their speed. A new hull design overcame this problem by using a completely new type of tunnel shape and the result was the fast slipway lifeboat which will increase the lifesaving capability at many slipway stations.

The prototype Medina lifeboat with an open steering position. The large tube gives great stability when the boat is at rest, or picking up survivors.

At Walton, Essex, the lifeboat is moored afloat and is reached by rowing out in a boarding boat (above left). The mooring chains and anchors are checked periodically by divers (above right).

Launching

There are three main ways of keeping lifeboats at their station, each accounting for about one third of the fleet. The easiest way is to keep the boat permanently afloat, moored to a buoy, and to reach it in a wooden or rubber dinghy, called a boarding boat. As lifeboats are on 24-hour call, the harbour or river estuary must not dry out at low tide and it must be possible to get away even in the worst weathers. Arun, Thames, Waveney and Clyde class lifeboats must be moored afloat, and many Watsons, Solents and Barnetts are kept this way. The disadvantage is

that weed grows on the hulls, which can also be rotted or eroded by seawater and the weather.

In exposed parts of the coast there may be high cliffs and no sheltered harbours so boathouses are built with slipways to launch the lifeboat into deep water. The lifeboat sits at the top of the slipway, held by retaining chains. When these are removed, the boat is held on one wire rope, attached by a quick-release hook. This is freed by releasing a locking screw and knocking the hook with a hammer, and the lifeboat races down the slipway to the sea, guided by the central groove. This is a fast, efficient method of launching, though recovery is more difficult as the lifeboat's stern is brought on to the slipway, a cable is attached and the boat is winched up backwards into the boathouse. In bad weather this can be impossible so the lifeboat may have to wait in the nearest harbour until the storm dies down. This means a long trip and may keep the lifeboat away from her station for a day or two.

In parts of the country, particularly on the east coast of England, there are beaches where the sea leaves long stretches of sand at low tide. Here the lifeboat must be pushed to the sea on a carriage.

Slipway launch at Cromer, Norfolk.

Specially waterproofed tractors are used though up to the 1930s teams of horses or people had to drag the boats into the water. The lifeboat is held on to the carriage with chains which are released before the boat is pulled into the sea by ropes which go around pulleys on the carriage and back to the tractor. Recovery is a complicated operation, involving dragging the lifeboat up the beach over skids and then hauling her on to the carriage, which tips forward to receive the boat and balances finely when its 8 ton load is back in place.

At two lifeboat stations, Walmer and Aldeburgh, none of the above methods is suitable. The shingle on the beaches shifts with every tide, so a slipway would be covered or eroded and a carriage might not be able to reach the sea. Instead the lifeboat sits at the top of the beach on a tipping cradle and skids are laid over the beach to form a pathway to the sea. The skids are greased wood or plastic planks and the boat slides over them when it has been pushed off its cradle. On return it is winched back up over the skids. This method used to be more common before tractors and carriages were available and in some small villages where there were only enough men to form the crew, the women turned out to launch the lifeboat, getting cold and soaked and waiting for hours for the boat to return.

Sheringham, Norfolk, lifeboat returns to the beach in stormy weather. The lifeboat is pulled up the beach over the skids and back on to her carriage. *Above left and right*

Filey, Yorkshire, lifeboat sits on her carriage facing the sea. The tractor and carriage have caterpillar tracks for driving over the beach and into the water. The retaining chains holding the lifeboat to the carriage are clearly visible. *Opposite*

Launching (above) and recovering (below) the Walmer lifeboat requires dozens of people. The movement of the shingle makes every launch slightly different.

Inflatables are launched off small trolleys which can be pushed to the sea by two or three people. The heavier Atlantic 21s have larger trolleys and when they are launched off an open beach a drive on, drive off (DODO) trolley is used. The Atlantic 21 sits in the trolley, with her engines running, allowing the helmsman to pick the right moment between waves to drive the boat out of the trolley. Coming back, a net is rigged on the trolley and the boat is driven straight into the net which collapses around the bow, holding the boat steady while flexible ropes are attached. The Atlantic 21 can be launched and recovered in heavy surf using the DODO and in extreme emergencies the lifeboat can be driven straight up a beach.

Maintenance

To keep lifeboats in top condition, a regular maintenance programme is worked out.

A motor mechanic is employed at each station with a large lifeboat, to look after the boat's machinery and check the equipment. He runs the engines at least once a week and undertakes routine maintenance. There is a back-up staff of marine engineers, mechanics, electronics engineers, and surveyors to deal with specialized or unusual repairs which can often be carried out at the station. If the boat is badly damaged or needs complete replacement of machinery she may have to be sent to a boatyard. A relief lifeboat will be sent to the station until the repairs are complete.

Relief boats are also used when the station lifeboat goes for her regular inspections and surveys. For boats kept in boathouses, provided routine inspections reveal no problems, there is a partial survey every four years and a complete survey every eight years. For boats kept afloat or on open beaches, however, there is an annual inspection, with some opening up of closed compartments in the second year, and partial and complete surveys at four and eight years respectively. A complete survey lasts for a period of months and involves a complete opening up of the boat. The engines, air cases where fitted and most of the other fittings and equipment are removed so that the structure of the boat can be examined in detail. The machinery is completely overhauled, new equipment may be fitted requiring rewiring, and the hull will be thoroughly inspected for dust, silt, rot or rust. The boat is finally reassembled, repainted and taken to sea on trials to ensure all is well.

Lifeboats have an average operational life of twenty-five to thirty years because of this careful maintenance.

A simple light trolley which is easily manhandled makes the launch
of the inflatable the quickest of any lifeboat.

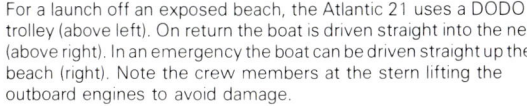

For a launch off an exposed beach, the Atlantic 21 uses a DODO trolley (above left). On return the boat is driven straight into the net (above right). In an emergency the boat can be driven straight up the beach (right). Note the crew members at the stern lifting the outboard engines to avoid damage.

Barnett

Hull material Wood
Introduced 1950
Length overall 15·9 m (52 ft)
Beam 4·3 m (14 ft)
Draft 1·4 m (4½ ft)

Displacement 29 tons
Maximum speed 9 knots
Range at full speed 216 nautical miles
Number of crew 7
Method of launching Down slipway or lies afloat

Watson

Hull material Wood
Introduced 14·3 m (47 ft) in 1956, 14·2 m (46¾ ft) Watson
   introduced in 1947
Length overall 14·3 m (47 ft)
Beam 4 m (13 ft)

Draft 1·3 m (4 ft 4 in)
Displacement 23·5 tons
Maximum speed Over 8 knots
Range at full speed 280 nautical miles
Number of crew 7
Method of launching Down slipway or lies afloat

D Class Inflatable
Hull material Nylon coated with neoprene
Introduced 1963
Length overall 4·72 m (15½ ft)
Beam 1·93 m (6 ft 4 in)
Draft Including engine 0·51 m (17 in)

Displacement 0·25 ton
Maximum speed 20 knots
Range at full speed 60 nautical miles
Number of crew 2/3
Method of launching From carriage or over beach

Clyde*
Hull material Steel
Introduced 1967
Length overall 21·3 m (70 ft)
Beam 5·4 m (18 ft)
Draft 2·5 m (8 ft 4 in)
Displacement 85 tons

Maximum speed Over 11 knots
Range at full speed 600 nautical miles
Number of crew 6
Method of launching Cruises or lies at moorings

*The statistics above are for the 70-001, the first of the type.

Waveney
Hull material Steel
Introduced 1967
Length overall 13·4 m (44 ft)
Beam 3·8 m (12½ ft)
Draft 1·2 m (4 ft)

Displacement 18 tons
Maximum speed Over 15 knots
Range at full speed 167 nautical miles
Number of crew 5
Method of launching Lies afloat

Solent

Hull material Steel
Introduced 1969
Length overall 14·8 m (48½ ft)
Beam 4·3 m (14 ft)
Draft 1·4 m (4½ ft)

Displacement 27 tons
Maximum speed Over 9 knots
Range at full speed 240 nautical miles
Number of crew 7
Method of launching Down slipway or lies afloat

Arun
Hull material Wood or glass reinforced plastic
Introduced 1971
Length overall 15·9 m and 16·5 m (52 ft and 54 ft)
Beam 5·2 m (17 ft)
Draft 1·5 m (5 ft)

Displacement 28·3 tons
Maximum speed 18 knots
Range at full speed 250 nautical miles
Number of crew 6
Method of launching Lies afloat

Atlantic 21
Hull material Glass reinforced plastic hull with neoprene sponson inflated
Introduced 1972
Length overall 6·9 m (22½ ft)
Beam 2·3 m (7½ ft)

Draft Including engines 0·76 m (2½ ft)
Displacement 1 ton
Maximum speed 29 knots
Range at full speed 70 nautical miles
Number of crew 3
Method of launching From carriage

Rother
Hull material Wood
Introduced 1973
Length overall 11·4 m (37½ ft)
Beam 3·5 m (11½ ft)
Draft 1·1 m (3½ ft)

Displacement 13 tons
Maximum speed Over 8 knots
Range at full speed 150 nautical miles
Number of crew 7
Method of launching Down slipway or from carriage or lies afloat

Thames
Hull material Steel
Introduced 1973
Length overall 15·3 m (50 ft)
Beam 4·4 m (14½ ft)
Draft 1·4 m (4½ ft)

Displacement 23·5 tons
Maximum speed 17 knots
Range at full speed 200 nautical miles
Number of crew 6
Method of launching Lies afloat

Medina
Hull material Wood with inflated neoprene sponson
Introduced 1980
Length overall 11·8 m (38½ ft)
Beam 4·3 m (14 ft)
Draft (out-drives down) 1·1 m (3½ ft)

Displacement 7 tons
Maximum speed 26 knots
Range at full speed 150 nautical miles
Number of crew 4
Method of launching Lies afloat; experiments with trolley due

73

Brede
Hull material Glass reinforced plastic
Introduced 1980
Length overall 9·9 m (32½ ft)
Beam 3·6 m (12 ft)
Draft 1·3 m (4 ft 4 in)

Displacement 8½ tons
Maximum speed 20 knots
Range at full speed 140 nautical miles
Number of crew 4
Method of launching Lies afloat

Fast Slipway Lifeboat
Hull material Steel
Introduced 1982
Length overall 14·1 m (46½ ft)
Beam 4·5 m (15 ft)
Draft 1·2 m (4 ft)

Displacement 24 tons
Maximum speed 15 knots
Range at full speed 226 nautical miles
Number of crew 6
Method of launching Slipway or can lie afloat

The fast slipway lifeboat undergoing self-righting trials.

Equipment

Every piece of equipment on a lifeboat must be sturdy, reliable, and as simple to operate as possible. Many traditional items are still carried: axes, boat-hooks, compasses, drogues. Other items which might seem redundant with modern electronic equipment available can be vital if that equipment fails, or can do jobs which electronics cannot; binoculars, signalling lamps, flares. As technology advances, better equipment is made to perform more functions, but it is only as good as the person who is using it, so training is vital. A collection of just a few items carried by a lifeboat shows why the boats are so expensive, for they must be fitted with the best gear. A stores depot at Poole carries all the spare parts a lifeboat may need and operates a 24-hour a day facility to ensure that they can be rushed to the coast as soon as they are needed. Some of the specialized items are described on the following pages.

Line throwing equipment

In calm weather a lifeboat can usually get close enough to a yacht to pass a rope by hand, or throw a heaving line (i) a rope with a weight on the end to carry it through the air. For large vessels, in rough

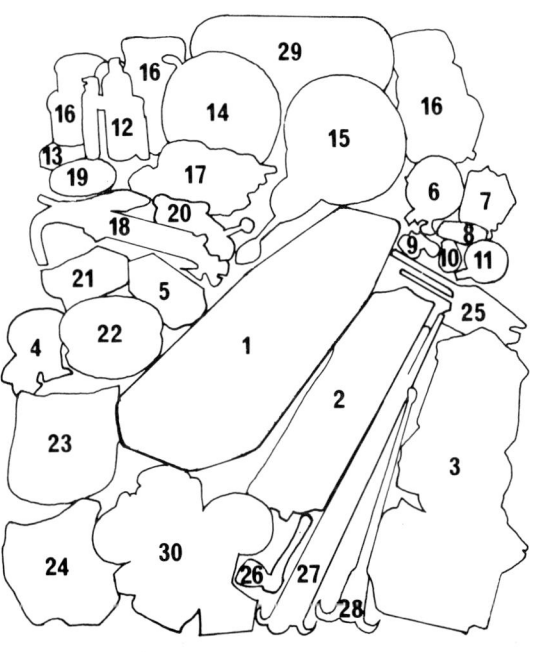

A selection of equipment carried in the modern lifeboat

1 Stretcher — Stokes Litter type
2 Stretcher — Neil Robertson type
3 Lifeboatman's protective clothing (lifejacket, bump cap, jersey)
4 Lifelines
5 First aid box
6 Searchlight
7 Line firing apparatus
8 Flares
9 Binoculars
10 Torch
11 Loud-hailer
12 Fire extinguishers
13 Fire hose
14 Breeches buoy
15 Drogue
16 Ropes
17 Fenders
18 Anchor
19 Anchor float line
20 Heaving lines
21 Canvas carrying sheet
22 Fresh air breathing apparatus
23 Swimmer's lifejacket
24 RNLI Ensign
25 Signalling flags
26 Axe
27 Boat hooks
28 Rope cutting tool
29 Liferaft
30 Emergency provisions

Line throwing equipment. *Above and opposite*

seas, or when boats are on rocks or sandbanks, the only way to make physical contact is by firing a line from a line gun (ii). The modern equipment consists of a yellow plastic drum containing the line, held by a handle which incorporates a trigger. When the trigger is pulled it fires a rocket 200 m (660 ft) through the air. The line attached to the rocket falls across the boat in trouble and when it has been caught a heavier rope can be hauled across. In this way a tow rope can be passed over, for although the lifeboat's job is only to save lives, in rough weather it can be safer to tow a boat to safety rather than to take the risk of injuring the survivors as they try to jump on to the lifeboat. Hundreds of boats are saved every year and salvage claims are virtually unheard of.

Breeches buoy

When people are stranded on a boat or on rocks and the lifeboat cannot reach them or tow their boat, they are rescued by breeches buoy. A line is fired and the breeches buoy equipment is then hauled over. The breeches buoy is a lifebuoy attached to a rope which runs through a pulley block. The block is attached to the casualty and each end of the rope running through it is held by the lifeboatmen. One by one, the survivors put the breeches buoy around their waists and they are hauled through the water to

Breeches buoy

the lifeboat, one group of lifeboatmen pulling the rope attached to the front of the buoy while another group pays out the back rope.

The operation must be carried out skilfully because in rough conditions the survivors must be brought to the lifeboat as quickly as possible and the job is made more difficult by gusts of wind blowing the rocket line off course and the danger of tangling the two breeches buoy ropes in rough seas.

Scrambling net

When people are in the water it is difficult to lift them up into the lifeboat so a net of strong rope, the scrambling net, is lowered into the sea. The lifeboatmen can use this to reach the people, who may be too weak to climb up the net. It can be seen hanging down by the man with the boathook retrieving a breeches buoy.

First aid

Every lifeboat crew has at least one first-aider. The injuries they deal with vary from minor cuts to broken backs and unconscious people needing mouth to mouth resuscitation. A very common condition among the people rescued is hypothermia, severe loss of heat from the body. This has several stages, leading to death and the chilling cold of the

Scrambling net

sea is probably responsible for more deaths than drowning. A pitching and tossing lifeboat is anything but the ideal place to carry out first aid but basic equipment carried by every lifeboat includes a first aid kit, blankets, a stretcher (being used here to transfer a man who had fallen down a cliff from the lifeboat's dinghy to the lifeboat) or carrying sheet and a special breathing tube for resuscitation when it is impossible to keep mouth to mouth contact. Conscious survivors are given hot drinks or, if they are not hypothermic, a nip of brandy. Lifeboats do not carry extensive provisions but powdered soups, tea and coffee, sweets, chocolate, biscuits and cigarettes are sufficient for most missions.

Doctors go out on rescues when it is known that somebody is seriously injured. The doctors, men and women, share the risks of the lifeboatmen and have the added danger of boarding large ships by climbing up rope ladders or even being hauled up on a rope.

Drogue

The greatest danger to a lifeboat is close to the shore where breaking waves are most powerful. If the

First aid   Drogue

lifeboat is caught broadside (sideways) on to a wave it can be rolled over as the wave breaks on to it and can capsize. It is therefore important to keep the lifeboat at right angles to the waves and this can be done by using a drogue, a tapering piece of canvas the shape of an ice cream cone with the end chopped off. The drogue is hauled through the sea behind the lifeboat and as the water passes through the narrowing cone of canvas it pulls at the drogue and the force keeps the lifeboat's stern pointing towards the breaking waves, preventing the boat from being swept around. Some modern lifeboats are fast enough to drive ahead faster than the speed of the waves and can avoid broaching but drogues are still used on the slower boats. The boats also carry storm oil which can cause a temporary calm if it is sprayed over a small area of sea. As the oil spreads it prevents the waves from breaking for a short time. This technique used to be common for going alongside wrecks or for the pulling lifeboats returning to the shore, towing a drogue and spreading the oil behind to try and stop the waves from breaking. Fish oil is used so no pollution is caused.

Electronic equipment

The cabin of an Arun with its knobs, dials and seats with seat belts looks more like the cockpit of an aircraft than the lifeboat coxswain's control centre. Instruments give him information on the engine revolutions, fuel, the charge in the batteries, a bank of switches controls the lights, while there are warning lights for the watertight doors and for fire. Two fire extinguishing systems are built into the engine room, one automatic and one activated from the cabin and individually shaped chocks can block off every air inlet to the engine room to help choke off the fire.

A mass of electronic equipment helps the coxswain with communication and navigation. This enables the lifeboats to find casualties much more quickly and has supplemented rather than replaced traditional items such as binoculars, Francis signalling lamps, flares and loud hailers.

The lifeboat's link with the shore is provided by radio. There is a radio frequency set aside for distress messages as well as a coastguard working frequency and as long as the casualty is fitted with radio, both the coastguard and lifeboat can be updated on its position and state.

Navigation is helped by radar, direction finder and Decca navigator.

Radar works by sending out electromagnetic waves from a revolving scanner. The waves are reflected back off anything they hit and are picked up

Electronic equipment in the wheelhouse of an Arun.

More electronic equipment!

again by the scanner, which passes them down a cable into a display unit. Images on a screen show the shapes and distances of objects such as cliffs, rocks and ships. Small boats of wood or glass fibre may not be picked up so most lifeboats carry a radar reflector which helps other ships' radar sets to pick them up.

The direction finder consists of two circular loops which are set at right angles. When radio signals are picked up, these loops can be used to tell the direction they are coming from, which is useful for navigation or for homing in on a ship which is transmitting the signals.

The Decca Navigator also picks up signals, but these come from special transmitters on the shore. A box of electronics works out which transmitters' signals are being picked up and how strong they are and from this information gives the coxswain a series of numbers which, when transferred to a grid on a special chart, pinpoints his position immediately.

Some lifeboats are also fitted with an automatic pilot which will keep the boat on a set course, automatically adjusting the rudders and relieving the coxswain of the job of steering on a long passage in open water. Closer into the shore he would have to take over and would be looking at his echo sounder which tells him the depth of water under the boat. In one rescue, when the coxswain had to drive over sandbanks to get to a casualty quickly, the echo sounder registered zero so the coxswain had it switched off!

Clothing and lifejackets

The lifeboatmen themselves need to be protected from the lashing spray, winds and rain they may meet. They have bright orange or yellow waterproof clothing which not only keeps them warm and dry but is also easily seen in case they should fall overboard. The RNLI uses special lifejackets packed with foam so that if a person should be knocked unconscious as he falls into the sea, he will float face upwards. There is a mouth tube so that air can be blown in to provide extra buoyancy. The lifejackets have a whistle, a light with a special sea water activated battery, reflective strips which will glow in the beam of a searchlight, a toggle for lashing survivors together, a lifting strap and a safety line which can be clipped to the lifeboat to prevent a person being swept overboard.

Training

The best training for lifeboatmen is to go to sea, so every six weeks, if there has not been a service

R.N.L.I LIFE-JACKET

Lifejacket

launch, the lifeboat has an exercise. If the coxswain wants to train new crew members, he will take them out on exercise to learn about the boat and her equipment. Every six months the lifeboat inspector for the area will take the crew out for a full exercise which includes an exhaustive check on the condition and use of equipment. The inspector will also arrange radar training courses for some crew members and when a station gets a new boat will go with the crew to the building yard for the passage back to station. About a third of lifeboat launches are in the dark, so the delivery trip of a new boat includes a night passage.

Lifeboatmen learn correct radio procedures in a mobile training unit, a caravan specially fitted out with desks and radio handsets. A training inspector drives the unit to the station and gives evening lessons for two weeks, when the crew are ready to take the examination for their radio operator's certificate.

First aid is usually taught by the lifeboat station's doctor or by the local St John Ambulance Brigade and many lifeboatmen learn lifesaving techniques from the Royal Lifesaving Society.

Lifeboats around the world

Over thirty countries in the world now have organized lifeboat societies; between them they operate well over 2,000 lifeboats of many different designs. Each lifeboat society is unique in its organization and its boats, for each country has a different coastline with its own problems and in many countries there were individual lifeboat stations before a national body was formed. The societies are linked by the International Lifeboat Conference (ILC) which acts as a means of exchanging information and ideas by an annual publication, *Lifeboat International,* and by holding conferences in different countries every four years. The RNLI provides the central administration of the ILC, as the first conference was held in London in 1924 to mark the RNLI's centenary.

International co-operation on lifeboat matters is widespread, the first recorded example being the use of eight of Henry Greathead's lifeboats in foreign countries, before any nation had even organized a lifeboat service. The RNLI was the first national service formed in 1824 and two lifeboat societies were established in the Netherlands in the same year. The Dutch used volunteer crews and voluntary financial support, and since then many countries have turned to the RNLI or the Dutch societies for advice. Rescue services in France, Sweden, Denmark, South Africa, Spain and Portugal were all modelled on the RNLI and when a service was established in the Netherlands Antilles in 1976, it used the principles of the RNLI and the Dutch societies combined with the methods of the United States Coast Guard Auxiliary.

In Europe, the lifeboat societies of Britain and Ireland, the Netherlands, Spain, Sweden and West Germany, all operate on a voluntary basis. They have all found the system to be the most efficient and economic for their countries and cannot see any way in which state aid would help them. Acting as independent bodies, these lifeboat societies have remained flexible and have developed exciting new lifeboats to meet changing needs. Voluntary crews also draw great moral support from the fund raisers.

The United States Coast Guard is the world's largest sea rescue organization and is run by the US Government. The USA's first lifeboat was provided by the Massachusetts Humane Society in 1807 and the US Lifesaving Service was formed in 1871. There was also a Revenue Service to prevent smuggling, which had a responsibility for lifesaving and in 1915 the two services were combined to form the Coast Guard. The US Coast Guard now has the job of providing lighthouses, lightships, buoys and beacons; keeping shipping lanes clear by using ice

The Netherlands has two lifeboat societies, one each for the north and the south of the country. Both were founded a few months after the RNLI and the links between the three organizations are very close. *Above left and right*

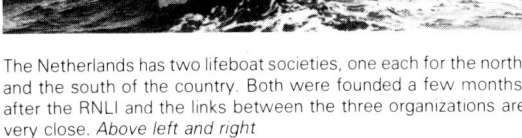

The United States Coast Guard 13·4 m (44 ft) steel lifeboat showing how she can operate in rough surf conditions.

92

Italy commissioned four RNLI Barnett class lifeboats to be built in
Cowes. This boat was built in 1964. Italy also uses German and
American designed lifeboats.

The Chilean lifeboat society is voluntary and describes the RNLI as
its 'spiritual mother'. The 14 m (47 ft) Watson stationed at
Valparaiso was bought from the RNLI.

breakers; running weather ships; law enforcement and search and rescue. Because the Coast Guard has so many tasks, it relies on full-time employees but it also operates an Auxiliary Service, composed of boat owners who volunteer their services to help with Coast Guard Work, using their own boats.

One of the US Coast Guard's boats, the 13·4 m (44 ft) fast lifeboat, has been used extensively by other countries. The RNLI version is the Waveney and these boats have been used in Canada, Portugal, Italy and Norway. Many RNLI designs have been used overseas and countries such as Australia, Belgium, Chile, Iceland, Italy, New Zealand, USSR and Turkey have all at some time bought RNLI lifeboats.

The RNLI's Atlantic 21 is used in the Netherlands and Portugal but it was the French who pioneered the use of small inflatable lifeboats which are now used throughout the world; even Switzerland has a lifeboat society, operating seventy-four boats on the Swiss Lakes.

Jet boats are also used for work close inshore, particularly in heavy surf or over reefs. Diesel engines provide the power to suck in sea water and force it out through jets, pushing the boat forward. There are no propellers to be damaged in the shallow water and the jets have the advantage of being able to turn almost immediately, even in bad conditions.

New Zealand's voluntary Sumner Lifeboat Institution shows its modern approach to lifesaving by using an all weather traditional lifeboat, *Rescue III,* a Liverpool class lifeboat bought from the RNLI, and a jet powered rescue craft *Aid II.*

This 9 m (29½ ft) jet rescue craft operated by the Bermuda Search and Rescue Institute was provided primarily as an air crash rescue boat but is also used for offshore sea rescue and is designed to work over coral reefs, where her jets are a great advantage over vulnerable propellers.

Pushed to the limits of her operational capabilities in angry surf, this South African jet rescue boat becomes almost airborne on a huge wave. The South Africans have built up considerable expertise with these boats and use plastic bottles in a net to provide buoyancy in case the boat is holed.

Their main disadvantage is that they need more powerful, and therefore heavier, engines than propeller driven boats. Jet lifeboats are used in New Zealand, Japan, Bermuda and South Africa.

Many lifeboat services develop boats to meet their own needs. In Norway and Sweden, for example, the fishing fleets spend weeks at sea and they are accompanied by a cruising lifeboat. These boats have living quarters for the crew, are centrally heated and are even fitted with an emergency surgery. Poland also has cruising lifeboats which can be used for salvage as well as saving life.

Two rescue cruisers from Scandinavia, the *Sigurd Golje* of Sweden
(left) and *R. S. Platou* of Norway, are both designed to accompany
their fishing fleets to sea.

In Germany the coast is flat with wide expanses of shallow water off the shore and sandbanks and islands riddled with thousands of shallow channels. Deep water lifeboats cannot navigate these channels so the Germans have developed large 44·5 m (146 ft) rescue cruisers that carry a daughter boat which launches from the stern. The success of the large cruisers led to the introduction of a smaller 16·8 m (55 ft) class of lifeboats which also carry a daughter boat. These German designs are also used in South Africa and Italy.

The Canadians use a hovercraft, based at Vancouver airport, to cover the Georgia Strait between Vancouver Island and the Mainland. It has the advantage of being able to skim over floating logs and ice found in this area and in fine weather has a maximum speed of 55-60 knots.

Helicopters and fixed wing planes are widely used for sea rescues. In Britain, the RAF flies sophisticated Nimrod reconnaissance jets, fitted with tracking radar and computers to home in on a casualty. A lifeboat or helicopter can then be directed to the spot and carry out the rescue. The Royal Navy and Royal Air Force now use twin engined Sea King helicopters in addition to the smaller Wessex and Whirlwind. These rugged aircraft can sometimes carry out rescues which lifeboats would find virtually impossible; from cliffs surrounded by rocks or from merchant vessels beyond a lifeboat's range. The co-operation between helicopters and lifeboats was shown in the 1979 Fastnet Race in which helicopters saved seventy-four lives, and thirteen lifeboats, spending a total of 186 hours at sea, saved another sixty lives.

In most countries it is the armed forces which operate helicopters. The US Coast Guard, however, has its own planes and helicopters. Here is convincing proof that both lifeboats and helicopters are needed, for if the USCG thought that aircraft could do all the work, they would not be developing new types of lifeboat. The trend which the RNLI has observed is that both helicopters and lifeboats are getting busier, and that they make a superb rescue combination in many cases.

The next stage in world-wide lifeboat development will be the formation of organized lifeboat services in the Third World countries. It is noticeable that all the rich countries of the world have lifeboat services but the fishermen and sailors of the Third World countries need just as much protection and saving lives at sea is an expensive business. It is to be hoped that the expertise which already exists in the rich nations can be passed on, perhaps with practical financial help, to the poorer ones.

This 15 m (50 ft) Danish lifeboat from Hvide Sande on the west
coast of Jutland has a speed of 9 knots.

Turkish lifeboats are financed by the Turkish Maritime Bank.

This fast sleek offshore rescue boat *Anne de Bretagne* is stationed at Le Croisic, France, and belongs to the Société Nationale de Sauvetage en Mer. *Above*

To deal with shallow water rescue, large German lifeboats carry daughter lifeboats which are launched from the stern of their mother ship. *Opposite*

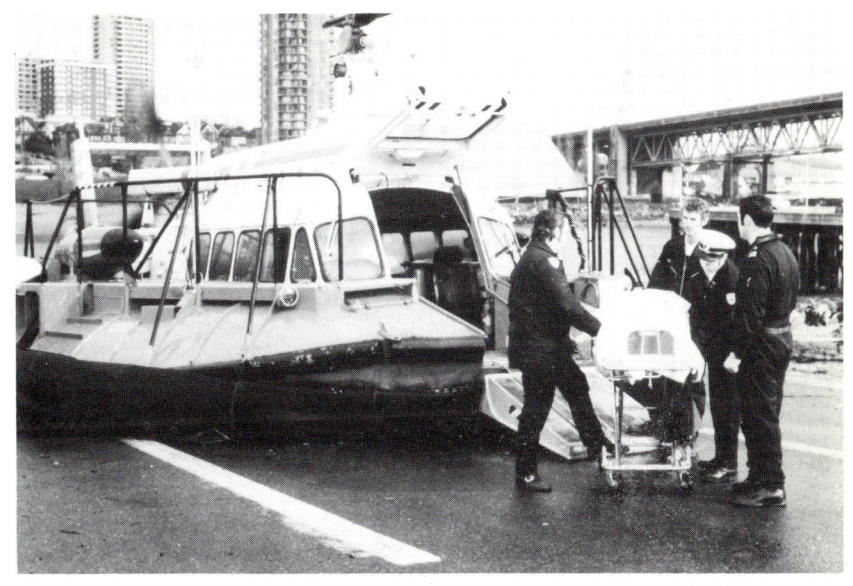

The German lifeboat the *John T. Essberger* is one of the most sophisticated in the world. She is 44·5 m (144½ ft) long, has an aluminium alloy hull and her three engines give a range of 966 km (600 miles) at 30 knots, or 9,660 km (6,000 miles) at 7 to 9 knots. Her daughter boat sits under a helicopter landing pad (marked with the letter H at the stern of the boat). *Left*

Landing an injured person from the world's only known rescue hovercraft operated by the Canadian Coast Guard and based at Vancouver Airport. *Above*

Inflatable lifeboats are widely used throughout Europe and this gathering is in Spain, where the lifeboat society is known as the Spanish Red Cross of the Sea, hence the emblem on the boats. The RNLI gave the society advice on its re-structuring in 1971.

The 18 m (60 ft) Japanese lifeboat *Jintzu Maru* has a speed of 11 knots. *Left*

People and rescues

Dozens of people are needed to run a lifeboat station. The most obvious, of course, are the coxswain and his crew. For lifeboats launched from a carriage, a slipway or across a beach, a team of shore helpers is needed with a head launcher in charge. Launching a lifeboat requires considerable skill and in rough weather the launchers must be alert for the coxswain's signal as he waits for a gap between the waves. The launchers must then wait for the lifeboat to return and recovery of the boat can also be a hazardous operation with the shore helpers often up to their waists in water.

A committee of volunteers deals with the administration of the station, the key post being the honorary secretary, usually a person with marine qualifications. The secretary decides whether the lifeboat should be launched and has deputies in case he should be away. Most of these jobs are done by men, though there are women honorary secretaries, launchers and crew members and at some stations the women used to form the main part of the launching teams. The RNLI is realistic in the rules it applies for joining a lifeboat crew. The applicant must pass a medical examination, must know about the sea or be willing to learn and must fit in with the other crew members. The last qualification is vital as the lifeboat crew works as a team with orders given by the coxswain or helmsman. There is no time for discussion in an emergency and orders must be carried out immediately and properly.

How a rescue works

There are four main organizations involved in search and rescue at sea in Britain, the RNLI, HM Coastguard, the Royal Navy and the Royal Air Force. In the Republic of Ireland, the RNLI provides the lifeboats, co-ordination is from a Marine Rescue Centre in Shannon and the Irish Armed Forces provide the helicopters.

Before a rescue can start, somebody must see or hear a distress signal. This can be a swimmer waving in panic, a red distress flare or a radio message broadcast on the frequency set aside for distress and received either by a Post Office Radio Station or a Coastguard. If a member of the public sees an accident at sea, a 999 telephone call to the coastguard will start the rescue. The coastguards are responsible for co-ordinating search and rescue. This means that as soon as they learn of an incident, they must decide how to deal with it, asking for the help of lifeboats, helicopters or other ships already at sea. The coastguards keep a watch from their cliff

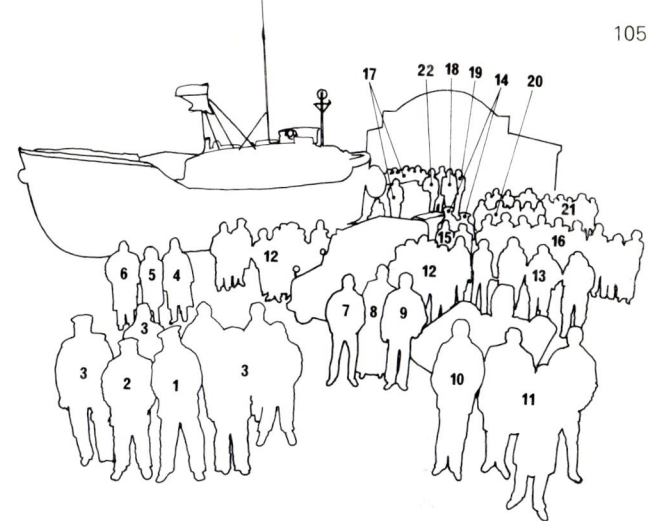

Wells lifeboat station

1 Coxswain David Cox
2 Second Coxswain Anthony Jordan
3 Oakley lifeboat crew
4 Lt David Case RNVR, station honorary secretary
5 Mrs David Case
6 Lt S. C. Long RNVR, deputy launching authority
7 Mr M. J. Hill, station honorary treasurer
8 Reverend David Chapman, chaplain
9 Dr D. W. Hoddy, honorary medical adviser
10 Lord Coke, president and patron
11 Branch committee representatives

12 HM Coastguards and Auxiliary Coastguards
13 Inflatable lifeboat crews
14 Police
15 Shipwrecked Mariners' Society
16 Life Guards
17 Launching crew
18 Brian Scoles, head launcher
19 Richard Woodgett, maroon firer
20 Ladies' guild committee members
21 Ladies' guild members
22 George Read, tractor driver

top look-outs in bad weather but have found that over 90 per cent of their calls come from radio messages or telephone calls. Because of this they have organized regional centres fitted with sophisticated radio and telex equipment. They need as much information as possible about the position of the casualty, the direction it is drifting, the number of people on board and the seriousness of the incident.

A lifeboat is usually required, so the coastguard telephones the honorary secretary of the lifeboat station, asking him to launch the boat. If he agrees, the honorary secretary summons the crew by firing two maroons, which explode with a loud bang and a flash. He may also telephone key crew members such as the coxswain, mechanic and head launcher. At some stations electronic bleepers are carried by the crew and they rush to the boathouse as soon as these are activated.

The coxswain will radio the coastguard as soon as the boat is afloat to get details of the casualty and, throughout the rescue, the lifeboat will pass messages to the coastguard who will inform the honorary secretary of the lifeboat's actions.

In many cases a helicopter is called and the coastguard will contact the relevant Royal Navy or Royal Air Force helicopter station. The biggest and most sophisticated helicopter used in search and rescue is the Sea King. This aircraft has twin engines and can fly at night or in fog using computerized navigation systems. Once in the air, Sea Kings have a much greater range and speed than lifeboats, so they are often used for taking injured seamen to hospital and for incidents far out to sea.

Working together, the lifeboats and helicopters can search huge areas and assist each other in rescues. When a freighter was sinking off Land's End in the storms of September 1981, it was the Sennen Cove lifeboat that arrived first but two of the survivors fell into the sea as they jumped for the lifeboat. The powerful searchlights of a Royal Navy helicopter pinpointed them until the lifeboat could pick them up. The helicopter went on to lift four men from a liferaft while the lifeboat rescued a total of seven.

The lifeboat returns to her station when the rescue is over but the work is not finished. The shore helpers re-house the lifeboat which must be washed down and re-fuelled, ready for immediate action if the call comes. This can take an hour or two and the

Blizzards do not deter the launch of the Bridlington lifeboat, as the crew and launchers take her down to the sea to escort three fishing vessels to safety.

Combined rescue: *Blue Peter III,* one of four inflatable lifeboats provided by the viewers of the famous BBC programme, took medical assistance to a boy who had fallen over a cliff near North Berwick. The bay could only be reached from the sea, but the boy was too badly injured to be taken out in the lifeboat so a helicopter was requested. HM Coastguard lowered extra medical equipment down the cliff. The RAF helicopter brought two doctors, lifted the boy and took him to Edinburgh hospital while the lifeboat took the helpers and equipment back to base. *Left*

The mighty Sea King. *Above*

In December 1974 the motor vessel *Biscaya* was badly damaged (above) when she collided with an oil rig under tow in the North Sea. The Great Yarmouth and Gorleston lifeboat was called out to stand by while a tug was called. The lifeboat waited for five hours in the gale and huge seas while desperate efforts were made to pump water out of the Biscaya but her list was increasing. Finally, six men were taken off the *Biscaya* only three minutes before she sank (below). Coxswain John Bryan won a bronze bravery medal for this rescue.

job is always done, day or night, so that the coast-guard can be told that the lifeboat is once again 'ready for service'.

Helicopters have established a major position in marine search and rescue over the past twenty-five years. Many of their services are in the same appalling conditions faced by lifeboats and helicopter pilots, crews and winchmen have displayed outstanding bravery on many occasions. But some hazards make helicopter rescue impossible as twelve Leith trawlermen discovered in 1974.

One night their trawler, the *Netta Croan,* caught fire when a blow back in her stove set the galley alight. It was impossible to extinguish the spreading flames and as the after end of the trawler burned fiercely, the trawlermen had to shelter on the forward part of their boat, away from the wheelhouse. The engines were still running at full speed so the trawler was sailing ahead at 9 knots, completely out of control.

The Greek ship *Nafsiporos* was adrift off Anglesey in tremendous storms in December 1966. The Holyhead lifeboat took off 5 men but the *Natsiporos's* lifeboat crashed down on her deck damaging the Holyhead boat. The Moelfre lifeboat then went in to save a further 10 men. Commander Harold Harvey, lifeboat inspector, at the wheel of the Holyhead boat and Richard Evans of Moelfre were awarded the RNLI's gold bravery medal.

A helicopter winchman made several attempts to get down to the deck but the flames and the erratic course made it impossible. He later said it was like trying to winch a Guy Fawkes off the top of a bonfire.

Meanwhile the Aberdeen lifeboat had been alerted, but with her top speed of 8½ knots she could only chase the burning trawler and as the lifeboat pursued her, the trawler started to circle. Coxswain Albert Bird decided to cut across her path, risking not only the possibility of being blown sky high if the fire reached the trawler's fuel tanks but also the chance that the trawler would change course again and collide with the lifeboat. As they got closer to the trawler the coxswain handed the wheel to Mechanic Ian Jack, a man who was experienced in taking moving boats together, while Albert Bird guided him towards the trawler. The lifeboat raced in at full speed, nudged the trawler and within a minute all twelve survivors had scrambled to safety. The men were landed in Aberdeen and the lifeboat set out again to search for a trawlerman who

Aberdeen lifeboat goes alongside the burning trawler *Netta Croan* while a helicopter illuminates the scene.

Coxswain Richard Evans of Moelfre won a gold medal for rescuing the crew of the *Hindlea* in 1958 by driving his lifeboat on to the deck of the ship.

had been lost overboard; after hours of looking he was given up as lost. Albert Bird and Ian Jack won silver medals for their bravery and skill.

In 1976 Aberdeen got a new Arun class lifeboat and in 1980, she was called out to help a helicopter returning from an oil rig with fifteen people on board which developed mechanical trouble and had to ditch in the sea. Another helicopter winched off eight survivors and the lifeboat towed the ditched helicopter into Aberdeen. It was an unusual service for a lifeboat, though other casualties have included submarines, planes, hovercraft, cows, a deer and a butterfly. Another unusual casualty, an oil rig, provided an excellent example of close co-operation between helicopters and lifeboats.

On 26 January 1978, the powerful ocean going tug *Seefalke* left Rotterdam towing the unwieldy 19,000 ton oil rig *Orion* on an 8,000 km (5,000 miles) journey to Brazil. The thirty-three men on the rig quickly settled into a routine for the long journey and after a week the two vessels were moving through the English Channel.

The night of February 1 was a dirty one, as north westerly gales swept the rolling Atlantic swells up

Aberdeen lifeboat tows the helicopter back to port while another helicopter takes off 8 of the survivors.

the Channel into short ugly waves. For the experienced men on the *Seefalke* and *Orion* it was nothing unusual. But the strain on the steel tow line became too much and the rig broke loose. The men on the tug fought to connect another tow while the rig drifted, helplessly, towards the treacherous reefs of Guernsey. At first it seemed the rig would be reconnected to the tug but as the storm force gales drove her on at 6 knots it became clear she would run aground.

St Peter Port lifeboat crew could see the rig, lights ablaze, racing towards the island. As they battled through the high seas to her aid they could make out the four legs of the rig towering 76 m (250 ft) above the waterline.

Coxswain John Petit, at the wheel of the lifeboat, feared the rig would strike the rocks and capsize. The Skipper of the rig lowered a scrambling net from his helicopter landing platform, 9 m (30 ft) above the waterline, but the net was far too long and trailed in the water, threatening to enmesh the lifeboat's propellers and leave her helpless. Time was running out as the dark shapes of the shore loomed up and Coxswain Petit started driving his lifeboat in as soon as he saw two men descending the net. His crew snatched one man to safety just as the net tangled with the lifeboat anchor and guard rails. The net

Dwarfed by the towering oil rig, the St Peter Port lifeboat manoeuvres amongst the rocks to get alongside and take off six salvage men in her second service to the *Orion*.

snapped taut, catapulted the other man into the sea and swept the lifeboat towards the rig. One of the lifeboatmen leapt into action and freed the net seconds before the seemingly inevitable collision. The coxswain immediately rammed his controls full ahead and went hard-a-port. At the same moment, however, a wave lifted the lifeboat towards the overhanging platform, smashing the mast and damaging the radar scanner. Nobody was hurt so the coxswain steered clear of the rig to pick up the man from the water. Just one minute later the rig ran aground.

Fortunately she settled on an even keel and, as helicopters were on their way, the lifeboat stood by for nearly four hours, tossing and pitching, while the pilots and winchmen performed seemingly impossible rescues of men from the rig. The fragile helicopter rotor blades were within inches of the rig's legs as the unrelenting wind blasted the airborne machines. Eventually the conditions became too dangerous for the helicopters so the lifeboat returned to St Peter Port, having spent 7½ hours at sea. The next day the remaining men were taken from the rig by breeches buoy but all was not over for the lifeboatmen. Nine days later, when a salvage crew was trying to float the rig off, she broke from her barge. The lifeboat put out once again in force 9

gales and snow storms to take the six men off. Manoeuvring between the grounded rig and the shore as the swell lifted and dropped the lifeboat was 'fairly routine' according to Coxswain Petit who was awarded the RNLI's silver medal for gallantry for the skill and courage he showed on the first rescue.

The Atlantic 21 lifeboat is designed to do many things. She can put to sea at night; she can be righted if she is capsized; she can carry twenty survivors and still squeeze in more; she can even be driven up on to a beach in an emergency. One thing her designers never thought of was driving her on and off the deck of a fishing vessel, yet that is exactly what helmsman Bev Brown of New Brighton did to rescue three men one night in 1974.

The alert came just before midnight and because of rough seas, whipped up by a force 6 wind, Helmsman Brown decided to take a crew of five instead of the usual three. After attempts to launch on the north side of New Brighton pier failed because of the heavy surf and difficulty in starting the port engine, the lifeboat was rushed by road to a more sheltered site a little to the south. Here the boat was successfully launched with both engines working. Ten minutes later she found the fishing vessel aground on a sandbank about 300 m (1,000 ft) from the beach and 350 m (1,150 ft) away from

New Brighton's Atlantic 21 lifeboat drives onto the deck of a fishing vessel to rescue three men.

dangerous rocks. She had an anchor out but was pitching and rolling in the rough seas and being pounded on the shore.

Helmsman Brown decided to anchor upwind of the vessel and veer down, helped by the wind and the tide. On the first attempt the lifeboat's cable proved too short and during the second attempt the casualty's anchor cable broke and she rolled towards a groyne. She was in immediate danger of breaking up so the lifeboat's cable was slipped and Helmsman Brown, driving at full speed, crossed the groyne on a large wave and drove his boat on to the fishing vessel's heavily listing deck. Two men were snatched off but there was a third man with an injured leg caught up in the rigging. Despite the fact that the fishing boat was now almost on top of the groyne lifeboatman Robin Middleton went aboard and struggling through the tangled ropes and fishing nets on the deck, dragged the injured man to safety. As the lifeboat left the fishing vessel, one of her propellers was fouled and had to be cleared while the boat was underway.

The injured man was handed over to waiting ambulancemen ashore and then the lifeboat returned to her station.

Bev Brown and Robin Middleton won silver medals for their bravery and the Atlantic 21 showed a new quality, though driving on to fishing vessels is not in the training programme!

Only one lifeboatman has ever been presented with the RNLI's gold, silver and bronze medals at the same time. He is Brian Bevan, coxswain of the Humber lifeboat, who earned his medals in a remarkable series of rescues in the winter of 1978-9.

The silver medal was awarded for rescuing six people, including a twelve-year-old girl from a listing Dutch freighter in December 1978. The rescue took place at night in storm force winds, with seawater freezing on the decks. As the lifeboat made for the casualty she crashed down off a huge wave, losing all her lights. The lifeboat crew had to use two hand torches to illuminate the scene as they grabbed the survivors.

Six weeks later, ferocious storms returned to the North Sea. Shortly before midnight in February the Panamian Coaster *Revi* was reported in trouble 48 km (30 miles) off Spurn. Her cargo of silver sand had shifted and she was listing dangerously. As soon as the Arun class lifeboat left the Humber Estuary she encountered huge seas, estimated at 11 m (35 ft) high. The *Revi* was slowly sinking and was trying to make for the River Humber. The lifeboat had to reduce speed because of the storm but still she pushed ahead at 14 knots, faster than any conven-

Humber lifeboat, *City of Bradford IV*, made over 30 runs in to rescue four men from the Panamanian coaster *Revi*.

Coxswain Brian Bevan, the only man ever to have been presented with the RNLI's gold, silver and bronze medals at the same time.

tional lifeboat, and but for this speed she would have been too late. Heavy seas were completely burying the *Revi* so that Coxswain Bevan first thought it would be impossible to take anybody off. As he made a trial run in, a sea hit the freighter and sent her menacingly towards the lifeboat, which went full astern. After a number of similar approaches, with the freighter often rising 6 m (20 ft) above the lifeboat's deck, two survivors were taken off. The

Revi's list increased and the captain decided that he and the mate would have to abandon ship.

The lifeboat crew, lashed to the rails, could see huge seas sweeping right along the freighter and it took twelve attempts to get alongside again. The mate jumped into the arms of the lifeboatmen who broke his fall and hurried him below.

The last survivor, the captain, was hanging on to the outside of the *Revi's* rails as the bows of his ship

Saved.

submerged and the stern loomed menacingly above the lifeboat. On the tenth attempt to get him off, the lifeboat approached and the *Revi* rose in the air and began to crash down towards the lifeboat's foredeck where the crew were lashed with no chance of escape. In a split second, Coxswain Bevan's instinct made him ram his throttles hard astern and the lifeboat's engines strained to pull her clear. The *Revi* crashed down, only inches away from the lifeboatmen; they were safe only because of the Arun's impressive power, but there was still one man to rescue. Death had stared the crew in the face and they knew that going in again could finish them. As the lifeboat was preparing for yet another approach, the *Revi* was completely covered by three successive seas and the captain was feared lost. However, when the water cleared, he was seen, still hanging on to the rails. Now there was no choice. The *Revi* was in immediate danger of rolling over. Somehow they had to save him.

Coxswain Bevan decided to dash in to the casualty in a trough between two waves. The lifeboat was driven in, striking the ship's stern and the captain jumped, almost fell overboard but was grabbed by the crew. A few minutes later the *Revi* rolled over and sank.

This rescue earned the gold medal for Brian Bevan

and bronze medals for each of his crew. Within 24 hours they were called out again, this time to a Romanian cargo ship. Wells lifeboat, an 11·3 m (37 ft) Oakley with an open cockpit, had put out to stand by the vessel in a force 12 hurricane, blizzards and 12 m (40 ft) waves and she stayed on the scene until the Humber lifeboat was on her way. The Wells boat was at sea for twelve hours, with the lifeboat crew up to their waists in water. As there was no cabin to protect them, the men soon felt the effects of the chilling cold which was so painful that one lifeboatman later said it would have been a relief to have been swept overboard and drowned. When they eventually returned to Wells the men had to be lifted out of the lifeboat and two of the crew did not recover the feeling in the tips of their fingers for three weeks. This was one of the most severe services in recent times and Coxswain David Cox was awarded a silver medal for his courage and tenacity.

Meanwhile the Humber lifeboat, with an enclosed cabin, had her own problems. Spray was freezing on the decks and 10 cm (4 in) of ice had to be chipped from the radar scanner. The lifeboat reached the freighter and escorted her to safety, a service lasting fifteen hours. Coxswain Bevan was awarded a bronze medal and earned a place in the history books for this remarkable series of rescues.

Bravery awards

The RNLI awards medals for bravery, the highest being the gold medal. It is awarded for 'an act in which outstanding courage, skill and initiative have been shown'.

The gold medal has been dubbed 'The Lifeboatman's VC' but is even rarer than the Victoria Cross; a total of 139 have been awarded since the foundation of the RNLI and there have only been 7 gold medals awarded for bravery since 1945. These were to Thomas King of Jersey; Richard Evans of Moelfre (2 medals); Hubert Petit of St Peter Port; Harold Harvey, RNLI Inspector; Keith Bower of Torbay and Brian Bevan of Humber.

Sir William Hillary was awarded a gold medal for founding the RNLI and won three more for exceptional rescues. This record was surpassed by Henry Blogg of Cromer, who won three gold and four silver medals.

The silver and bronze medals are awarded for outstanding acts of bravery which do not meet the requirements for the gold.

Each medal is accompanied by a certificate giving details of the service and many of these can be seen in boathouses or lifeboatmen's homes.

A certificate of thanks, inscribed on vellum (a

parchment made of animal skin) is the award below the bronze medal.

All the bravery awards are carefully considered by an RNLI Committee and out of over 2,500 rescues each year an average of less than ten will result in medals.

Fund raising

The vital job of fund raising is carried out by some 2,000 branches of volunteers throughout Britain and Ireland. This army of supporters organizes thousands of functions such as dances, fetes, sponsored events, sales, auctions and, of course, the traditional lifeboat flag days. The RNLI was the first charity ever to organize street collections in 1891, though flags were not introduced until the 1920s. Modern fund raising includes appeals to industry, the sale of carefully selected gifts and souvenirs, collections of foreign coins and stamps and the RNLI runs its own lottery. Legacies bring in a substantial income and the membership scheme 'Shoreline' gives people the chance to make regular subscriptions. Schools, clubs, societies and individuals can all support the RNLI.

Details on souvenirs and gifts, local branches, Shoreline membership and the lottery are available from:

The Appeals Secretary
RNLI
West Quay Road
Poole
Dorset, BH15 1HZ

RNLI museums and display centres

Name	Location	Contents	Opening Times
Portpatrick	Old Lifeboat House	General display including a model of *The Original*.	Weekends during summer, variable during week, open on request for parties.
Dunbar	Lifeboat House	General display including present 'D' class lifeboat.	Weekends during summer, variable during week, open on request for parties.
Grace Darling Museum	Bamburgh Northumberland	Items relating to the life of Grace Darling including the coble in which Grace Darling and her father went to the aid of the *Forfarshire*.	Daily during summer.
Whitby	Old Lifeboat House	General display particularly as relevant to Whitby including the *Robert & Ellen Robson* the last pulling lifeboat on active service.	Daily during summer, open on request for parties during winter.
Cromer	Old Lifeboat House	General display including special display on the life of Henry Blogg.	Daily during summer, open on request for parties during winter.
Southwold	The Old Water Tower	Items relating to Southwold lifeboat history.	Afternoons during summer.
Harwich	Old Light Tower	Items relating to Harwich lifeboat history.	Weekends during summer.

Eastbourne	Lifeboat Museum The Promenade	General display particularly as relevant to Eastbourne—includes one of the few remaining cork lifejackets.	Daily during summer.
Shoreham	Display room adjoining Lifeboat House	Items relating to Shoreham lifeboat history.	Open on request throughout the year.
Poole	Head Office RNLI	Models and paintings relating to RNLI history.	9.00 a.m.—5.00 p.m. weekdays throughout the year—not Public Holidays.
Poole	Old Lifeboat House Fisherman's Dock	The *Thomas Kirkwright* lifeboat.	Daily during summer months.
St Peter Port	The Castle Cornet Museum St Peter Port, Guernsey	Display relating to history of St Peter Port Lifeboat station.	Daily throughout the year.
Exmouth	Lifeboat House	General display including present 'D' class lifeboat.	Daily during summer.
Clovelly	Old Lifeboat House	General display particularly as relevant to Clovelly including large model of present 70 ft lifeboat.	Daily during summer.
The National Lifeboat Museum	Princes Wharf, Bristol	A growing display including several examples of old lifeboats and lifeboat equipment.	Weekends during summer.
Barmouth	The Town Museum	General display including model of the Rhyl tubular lifeboat.	Daily during summer.
Redcar	Zetland Lifeboat Museum	The *Zetland,* the oldest surviving lifeboat in the world.	Daily during summer.

Index

Source Books

Aircraft
Armoured Fighting Vehicles
Buses
Commercial Vehicles
Dinghies
Helicopters and Vertical Take-Off Aircraft
Hydrofoils and Hovercraft
Industrial Past
Locomotives
London Transport
Military Support Vehicles
Miniature and Narrow Gauge Railways
Motor Cars
Motorcycles
Naval Aircraft and Aircraft Carriers
Ships
Small Arms
Submarines and Submersibles
Tractors and Farm Machinery
Trams
Twentieth Century Warships
Underground Railways
Vintage and Post Vintage Cars
Windmills and Watermills
World War 1 Weapons and Uniforms
World War 2 Weapons and Uniforms